THE DANCE IN CHRISTIANITY

The Dance In Christianity

Marilyn Daniels

PAULIST PRESS
New York/Ramsey

Library of Congress
Catalog Card Number:
81-80048

ISBN:
0-8091-2381-9

Published by Paulist Press
545 Island Road
Ramsey, N.J. 07446

Printed and bound in the
United States of America

Contents

*for my children
Marc, Lisa and David
and all the world's children
for whom history is written*

A pre-Christian depiction of the dance of death,
seen on a beaker found near Pompeii. The
beaker is dated around 30 A.D.

Beginnings

Dance as an expression of man being moved by the transcendent power is the earliest art form; before man expresses his experience of life through materials he does so with his own body. It is probable that liturgical praying and ritual dancing coexisted in very early times, and it is also probable that the spoken drama and the musical dance have developed from worship—from liturgy on the one hand and ritual on the other.[1]

How much the dance was part of the life of biblical man is borne out by the many references to dancing in the Old Testament. There are three types of dance referred to: the processional dance, the encircling dance, and the ecstatic dance.

Biblical man was not very different from primitive man. His movements are not bent on harmonic effects. They come from a state of joy or sadness, of frenzy or ecstasy. This must have been the kind of convulsive dance referred to in Exodus when Moses came into the camp and saw the people dancing around the golden calf. When Moses took the calf they had made and burnt it in the fire, he turned against the god of gold, against the idol, not against their way of praising it.

After the crossing of the Red Sea, when the prophetess Miriam, the sister of Aaron, took a timbrel in her hand, all the women went out after her with timbrels and with dances. And Judith led a great chorus of women crowned with olive wreaths.

The most outstanding example of a principal dancer being followed and probably greatly imitated by the others was King David. In a religious procession organized in honor of Yahweh such as the removal of the Ark, David, dressed in the official robe of the high priest, danced in ecstasy before the deity. It was a rotary dance rich in gesture accentuated by violent leaps.[2]

> And David danced before the Lord with all his might; and David was girded with a linen ephod. . . . And as the Ark of the Lord came into the city of David, Michal, Saul's daughter, looked through a window, and saw King David leaping and dancing before the Lord (2 Sam. 6:14–16).

We have further references to Hebrews dancing in the Psalms.

> Let them praise his name with dancing,
> making melody to him with timbrel and lyre (Ps. 149:3).

> Praise him with timbrel and dance (Ps. 150:4).

> Thou hast turned for me my mourning into dancing;
> thou hast loosed my sackcloth and girded me with gladness (Ps 30:11).

In these passages in the Old Testament in which religious dancing is recorded there is no hint of disapproval. It is therefore evident that it must have been looked upon as a usual and integral part of worship. There are forty-four words in the Hebrew language for dancing and only once is there a possible reference to secular as distinct from religious dancing.[3]

Hebrew dance was a fusion of Semitic-Arabic and Babylonian forms. The most frequently used root in the Old Testament is "hul"; it expresses the whirl of the dance, and implies highly active movement. It would be one of the words spoken to describe the Kadish, an ancient Hebrew ritual dance known as "Holy." This dance's basic form was a circle plus square. There were twelve positions on the circumference of the circle each representing a patriarch or one of the twelve tribes; later there were the twelve apostles. The dancers would rotate as they circled round. "Karar" was the Hebrew word for this rotation movement.[4]

Their most celebrative dances were those done at the times of festivals. Within their agriculturally based society the three principal ritual festivals were Massoth or the Passover, Succoth or the Feast of Weeks (which was later to become Pentecost), and Tabernacles or the Feast of Booths.

The Jewish prophets danced in their communion with God. They danced before conveying the word of the Lord to the people, the symbolism of movement being more soul-stirring than words. Today we know that movement precedes speech. Rudolf Laban in *The Mastery of Movement* states: "Words expressing feelings, emotions, sentiments or certain mental and spiritual states will but touch the fringe of the inner responses which the shapes and rhythms of bodily actions are capable of evoking."[5] Before our tongue and lips can form the word, our arms, hands and face, obeying the commands of our thought-feelings, paint them through the involuntary expression of movement.

There is within man a common impulse to resort to these movements to externalize states which he cannot externalize by rational means.

Movement symbols are elemental and universal as a

means of communication between persons. They are more potent than symbols that are projected into the other arts. Ideas and sentiments are expressed by the flow of movement and become visible in gestures. Symbolic movements "speak" with direct and immediate communication.

The term "symbol" means basically to bring together. The function of a symbol is to bring together various relationships into a simple whole, to make something more meaningful through this relationship and to gather significance for members of a group so that they understand what the symbol represents. Paul Tillich wrote that a symbol opens "levels of reality which otherwise are hidden and cannot be grasped in any other way."[6]

No area of communication is more dependent on symbolic expression than is religious experience. The close connection between religious feeling and expressive movement, the dance, has been coeval with the history of man.

The Early Church

Christianity grew out of a strong Hebrew tradition with its use of the dance as a natural, spontaneous and accustomed way for people to express themselves in praise. The beginnings of the liturgy of the Christian worship were found in the service of the synagogue. The litany, the versicle and response, and the psalm or hymn are three historical forms which still keep their place in the liturgies of the Church.[7] The Hebrew psalter provided a rich source for religious expression. Dance was used in the order of worship of the two earliest Christian liturgies recorded in detail. Justin Martyr (A.D. 150) and Hippolytus (A.D. 200) both describe joyful circle dances.[8]

The New Testament has no direct reference to religious dance, although there was no aversion in the early Church to the use of the dance as an accepted expression of joy. We have a remark of Jesus, "We piped to you and you did not dance" (Mt. 11:17), which indicates that Jesus recognized dancing as a normal means of expressing joy. When he relates the story of the prodigal son he mentions that there was dancing and rejoicing over his return (Lk. 15:25).

The early Christians are reminded by Paul that their bodies are temples of the Holy Spirit and that they should glorify God with their bodies as well as their spirits (1 Cor. 6:19–20). In his letter to Timothy he shows that physical movement was an approved part of prayer expression: "I desire then that in every place the men should pray lifting holy hands" (1 Tim. 2:8).

There may be more references to dance in the New Testament than was originally thought. Recent studies suggest that "rejoice" and "dance" are the same word in the Aramaic language that Jesus and the disciples spoke. When you substitute dance for rejoice, you have Jesus saying "Dance and leap for joy" (Lk. 6:23) or "dancing in the spirit" (Lk. 10:21).[9]

Dating from about the year 120 there exists in the apocryphal Acts of John a remarkable hymn, quoted in the Catholic dictionary as being known to Augustine. It describes an incident at the Last Supper, where Christ, taking leave of his disciples, instituted the custom of Holy Communion, the symbolic basis of the Roman Christian religion and the source of the Catholic Mass. But here, instead of the breaking of bread and sipping of wine testifying to the oneness of Christ's body and blood, we have dancing.

> Now before he was taken by the lawless Jews, he gathered all of us together and said, "Before I am delivered up unto them let us sing a hymn to the Father, and so go forth to that which lieth before us." He bade us therefore make, as it were, a ring, holding one another's hands, and, himself standing in the midst, he said, "Answer Amen unto me." He began then to sing a hymn and to say: "Glory be to the Father." And we, going around in a ring, answered him: Amen. "Glory be to thee, Word: Glory be to thee, Grace." Amen. "I would be saved, and I would save." Amen. "Grace danceth. I would pipe; dance ye all." Amen. "I would mourn: lament ye all." Amen. "The number eight singeth praise with us." Amen. "The number twelve danceth on high." Amen. "The whole on high hath part in our dancing."

Amen. "Who so danceth not knoweth not what cometh to pass. I would be united and I would unite." Amen. "A door am I to thee that knocketh at me." Amen. "Now answer thou unto my dancing. Behold thyself in me who speak, and seeing what I do, keep silence about my mysteries. Thou that dancest, perceive what I do, for there is this passion of the manhood, which I am about to suffer. For thou couldst not at all have understood what thou sufferest, if I had not been sent unto thee, as the word of the Father. Thou that sawest what I suffer sawest me as suffering, and seeing it thou didst not abide but wert wholly moved. Who I am, thou shalt know when I depart. Learn thou to suffer, and thou shalt be able not to suffer. I would keep tune with holy souls. Do thou understand the whole, and having understood it, say: Glory be to the Father." Amen. Thus having danced with us the Lord went forth.

The steps to this particular dance have been lost, but we do have recorded a similar ancient dance of the Andamanese. It too is an imageless circle dance. The magical goal of the imageless exhilaration dance is the attainment of a state of ecstasy in which the dancer transcends the human and physical and, released from his self, wins the power of interfering with the events of the world. The circle stands for itself; it is closed to the surrounding world and to spectators, just as the ecstatic peoples are closed to the outside and are introverted. The circle later takes on a spiritual significance. This is not the result of a development of understanding but rather of the connection between an idea and its motor reflex: to encircle an object is to take it into possession, to incorporate it. The circle may be without a central point, or it may have as its center a person, as in the "Hymn of Jesus," whose power is supposed to radiate to those in the circle.

This is a description of the imageless dance of the Andaman Islands. Each dancer circles in whatever direction and executes whatever movements he pleases regardless of the others, although he always keeps strictly in time with the music. He hops lightly on his right foot, raises his left, lowers it and steps left. The trunk is flexed at the hips; the back is somewhat rounded. The arms are stretched forward shoulder high and both thumbs and pointer fingers are hooked. With this movement and posture they dance a short while in one place, then move on around the circle. Now and then a dancer adds of his own accord another variety of step to his dance.[10]

In *The Sacred Dance in Christendom*, G. R. S. Mead says that this hymn dance is an ancient mystery ritual of early Christendom.[11] As part of the apocrypha, the "Hymn of Jesus" was not included in traditional Christian literature, but it is nonetheless significant, since it illustrates that this type of dance was a part of the religious expression of the early Church.

The writings of the Christian Church, which were largely in Greek, often included the term "choros" and the plural "choroi." This is a Greek word for choral dances. It was believed by the Greeks that the dance provided a special way of expressing the overflow of awareness for which they had no words. This choral dancing had a particular dignity and beauty of harmonious movements. The classic Greek dramas used choral dances to emphasize a mood or reveal a hidden meaning.

One of the most sublime illustrations of sacred dancing in the early Church is quoted by Eusebius, the father of Church history.

> After the banquet they keep the sacred all-night festival.
> And this is how they keep it. They all stand up in a body,
> and in the middle of the banqueting-place they first form

two choroi, one of men and the other of women, and a
leader and conductor is chosen for each, the one whose
reputation is greatest for a knowledge of music; they
then chant hymns composed in God's honor in many me-
ters and melodies, sometimes singing together, sometimes one choros beating the measure with their hands
for the antiphonal chanting of the other, now dancing to
the measure and now inspiring it, at times dancing in
procession, at times set-dances, and then circle-dances
right and left.[12]

Another example of dance in the early Church is taken
from a Palm Sunday sermon of Epiphanius, who was bishop
of Salamis on Cyprus in 367. The festival of celebration is
described in these words.

Rejoice in the highest, daughter of Zion! Rejoice, be
glad and leap boisterously, thou all-embracing Church.
For behold, once again the King approaches. . . . Once
again perform the choral dances . . . leap wildly, ye heavens; sing hymns, ye angels; ye who dwell in Zion, dance
ring dances.[13]

Those who have interpreted this work conclude that it
describes not only the spirit of the ceremony, but also literal
dances done within the Church. This view is supported by
the writings of Basilius, bishop of Caesarea, who lived between 344 and 407. Basilius wrote frequently of the exis-
tence of the dance in the time of early Christianity, including
one passage which suggested that pagan rites such as dawn
ceremonies which greeted the sunrise were also found in the
early Catholic Church.

Could there be anything more blessed than to imitate on
earth the ring-dance of the angels and at dawn to raise

our voices in prayer and by hymns and songs glorify the rising Creator?[14]

This sacred dancing took place in the choir above, with the bishop in the role of leader. The idea of heavenly beings encircling the throne of God and singing his praise goes back to the Talmud, where dancing is described as being the principal function of the angels. In early Christian times it was supposed that during divine service, especially at Mass, the angels were present in the choir participating together with Christ in the performance of the Mystery. Christian iconography has, throughout the centuries, amply illustrated this notion of the singing and dancing angels.

Ambrose, the bishop of Milan in the late fourth century, wrote profusely in support of Church dance, taking his text from Luke 7:32, "We have piped unto you and ye have not danced."

A simple speech, but by no means a simple mystery! And for that reason we must be careful not to be snared into a commonplace interpretation of this speech and suppose that we can abandon ourselves to the actor-like movements of indecent dances and to the romance of the stage; such things should be regarded as dissolute, even in youth. No, the dance should be conducted as did David when he danced before the ark of the Lord, for everything is right which springs from the fear of God. Let us not be ashamed of a show of reverence which will enrich the cult and deepen the adoration of Christ. For this reason the dance must in no wise be regarded as a mark of reverence for vanity and luxury, but as something which uplifts every living body instead of allowing the limbs to rest motionless upon the ground or the slow feet to become numb. . . . But thou, when thou comest to the font, do thou lift up thy hands. Thou art exhorted to show swifter feet in order that thou mayest thereby ascend to the everlasting life. This dance is an ally of faith and an honoring of grace. The Lord bids us dance, not merely with the circling movements of the body, but with pious faith in him. . . . And just as he who dances with his body, rushing through the rotating movements of the limbs, acquires the right to a share in the round dance, in the same way he who dances the spiritual dance, always moving in the ecstasy of faith, acquires the right to dance in the ring of all creation.[15]

History tells us of many other early Church leaders who clearly supported and encouraged the dance. In the third century Bishop Gregory Thaumaturgus conducted dances and holy pantomimes within the space of the choir.[16] A century later Chrysostom, archbishop of Constantinople, who was fond of dancing himself, commends a Whitsun festival celebrating the descent of the Holy Spirit using these words:

Of those in heaven and those upon the earth a unison is made, one general assembly, one single service of thanksgiving, one single transport of rejoicing, one joyous dance. You danced those spiritual dances which are most modest; you circled and used musical instruments of the spirit, revealing your souls as do the musical instruments on which the Holy Spirit plays when he instills his grace into your hearts.[17]

Chrysostom advises his parishioners to dance to the glory of God. He uses David's dances as an example and refers them to pictures which illustrate David surrounded with his choroi of prophets singing, playing, and dancing. They are however warned not to use "unseemly motions," but to employ decent gestures. He urges Christians to keep their dances sacred, reminding them that God has not given them feet to use in a shameful way as the pagans do but that they should dance with the angels.

Augustine, another of the early Christian Church leaders, also cautions against dances which are not disciplined. While speaking against dances that are frivolous or unseemly, however, he endorses the dance in many of his writings, particularly for sacred festivals. He sees the sense of harmony in the dances and the need for this spiritual harmony in the participants.

> For what is the meaning of dancing if it is not to harmonize the bodily movements with song? . . . Be ye harmonious yourselves in your habits as are the dancers in the movements of their limbs.[18]

Theodoret, an eminent theologian of the fourth century, conceived of the sacred dance as a dance of the virtues in harmony with the powers above. Dancing in the heavens was the occupation of the angels. He saw them in their dance in the indestructible aeons. Theodoret urged his readers to follow the angels' example so that they might share in this dance.

The "Song of the Blessed Children" in Daniel 3 is generally associated with the salvation of those in the fiery furnace. Theodoret writes:

> They summon to the dance both heaven and the waters above the heavens, and the powers that circle round the divine throne. The flames of the burning fiery furnace are turned into dew so that those blessed children danced the dance in their midst, and sang the hymn. You too have been promised the kingdom of the heavens, and life that hath no end, and light intelligible, and to dance in company with those free of all body.[19]

The first five centuries of the early Church found dance being used by the people as part of their order of worship. It was a form of communication that they understood and that carried meaning for them. The liturgy has always reflected the ways in which man has attempted to commune with God. These early Christians were comfortable using dance to express their joys and their sorrows, their longings and their thanks. They were used to using their bodies and the dance as instruments of prayer and praise.

The Church danced during regular worship. There was particular emphasis placed on the dances done during the annual Church celebrations of Passover and Easter, Pentecost and later Epiphany. The people also danced outside the church at harvest festivals, rites of initiation, and various rites of passage. It was to these kinds of dances that Bishop Ambrose and others referred when they admonished the people against indecent dancing. The Church leaders supported and encouraged the use of dance as an ally of faith when it was done in the manner of Jesus.

There had been a natural fusion of sacred dance with the pagan ritual rites, and even at this early time in the history of the Christian liturgy we find attempts to separate the two. Within the ancient Church there began a gradual but decisive triumph of the liturgic over the spontaneous element in the common worship.

The Middle Ages

The countryside of the early Middle Ages was dotted with small villages, each containing about two hundred and fifty adults and one hundred and fifty children with no formal education. The church was their source of schooling and community. The clergy were a body better educated and more personally respectable than their average parishioners. It is estimated that they made up one in thirty of the population. The villagers were at home within the church and the difficulty was to prevent too great a familiarity. The towns were ostensibly the same when dealing with the subject of ecclesiastical influence.

The church councils started to forbid beer-drinking within its walls and prohibit markets in the church yard. Certain of the dances were looked on as too secular and began to be opposed. An example of this is the edict by the Council of Toledo forbidding dancing in the churches during the vigil of saints' days. This same Council of Toledo seems to have shifted its opinion in 678, when it suggested that Archbishop Isidore of Seville compose and present a ritual that would be rich in sacred choreography.

This ritual was incorporated into a Mass known as the Mozarabe and presented in the seven churches of Toledo. The first accounts of the dance as performed in the seventh century describe a wooden arc of the Testament carried through the cathedral in procession, accompanied by choirboys and priests. They were preceded by eight boys dancing and singing, and dressed as angels with garlands of flowers in their hair. It was discontinued in six of the churches during the middle of the fifteenth century, but is still celebrated three times each year in the Cathedral of Seville on Shrove Tuesday, the Feast of Corpus Christi, and the Feast of the Immaculate Conception.

This dance had a dramatic time in 1439 when Don Jayme de Palafox, the archbishop of Seville, forbade its performance. Amazed at this ruling the people of Seville collected enough money to send the young dancers to Rome where they performed before the Pope with singing, dancing, and the clicking of castanets. It is reported that Pope Eugenius IV said, "I see nothing in this children's dance which is offensive to God. Let them continue to dance before the high altar."[20]

The Mozarabe is described by Claes Lagergren, who attended the Mass in Seville in 1878:

Ten choristers entered, dressed magnificently as pages of the seventeenth century. Standing before the high altar, first they dropped on their knees, then they rose and sang a curious melodious song:

We believe in the bread of life
From Christ to our overflowing joy;
By our dance we supplicate him,
As once the Baptist supplicated.

Therefore by this dance
We strengthen our firm faith,
All to the sounds of music.

Then they put on hats, divided into two groups, and
stepped backward and forward, making figures and singing, sometimes accompanying themselves with castanets.
The dance lasted about a quarter of an hour and made
a very remarkable spectacle. The deep reverence of the
spectators emphasized the strangeness of the performance.[21]

The dance as it is performed today before the high altar in
the Cathedral of Seville is essentially the same dance that Lagergren described. At vesper-time ten boys dance before the
kneeling cardinal, archbishop, and clergy. They are accompanied by the cathedral organ and string orchestra with music in the Sequidilla rhythm. The music is $3/4$ or $3/8$ time,
usually in the minor key. In a Spanish-Moorish dance mode
of solemn measure, the dance is grave and dignified, without
much movement of arms or body. Each of the ten figures has
a mystical meaning, the most notable being simple and double chains in the figure 8 and double S-SS. At times a circle
is formed, or they create double lines, meet and cross, and
reassemble at right angles. They chant, sing and play castanets—a smaller type than usual, made of ivory and worn on
the middle finger instead of the thumb. They wear red
knickerbockers and tunics for Shrove Tuesday and Corpus
Christi and blue for the Feast of the Immaculate Conception.
Lace collars and cuffs adorn their tunics, and their plumed
hats are either red or blue damask, lined with white. In this,
its present form, the dance dates from 1264.[22]

The eighth and ninth centuries found sacred dances continuing to spread throughout Europe. At the same time the
Church tended to become more authoritarian and started to
regulate all forms of liturgical and church-related activities.
When the dance was virtuous and performed in the honor of
God, it was praised. When it appeared to be pagan or degenerate, the Church sought to restrain it.

Labyrinth in Chartres Cathedral.
(Drawing from J. Gailhabaud's *L'Architecture
du Ve au XVIIe siecle*, 1858.)

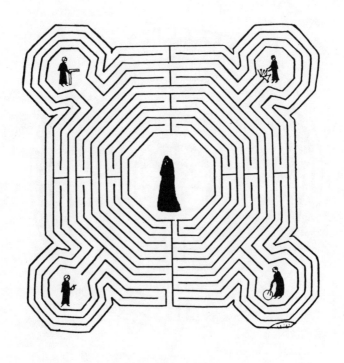

Labyrinth in Reims Cathedral.
(Drawing, Bibliotheque Nationale, Paris.)

The Flagellants appeared in northern Italy in the eleventh century and spread to Germany and later to Spain and England. People of all ages and classes formed long processions which were headed by priests carrying crosses and banners. They walked through the streets in double file reciting prayers and drawing blood from their bodies by whipping themselves and each other with leather thongs. These exhibitions, symbolic of repentance, were suppressed somewhat, but have reappeared occasionally throughout the centuries in various countries, including Mexico and the United States.[23]

There is a reference in a hymn of the second century to a labyrinth dance: "wandering in the labyrinth of ills." However, for the most part Church labyrinthine dances date from the eleventh century. The famous Cathedral of Chartres was constructed in 1200, and even today parishioners practice the devotion of the rosary on the labyrinth.

Labyrinths are to be found in many of the cathedrals and churches of Europe, inlaid in the floor of the nave near the west door. They were conceived of as three-dimensional, with the center or top being the heavenly Jerusalem. From early Christian times the sun was a symbol for Christ as the Sun of Righteousness, risen for all who dwell in darkness, a belief which is connected with the early medieval mystics' idea of the resurrected Christ dancing forth from the underworld.

The following inscription is carved on stone from a labyrinth, preserved in the Lyons museum: "Look upon this mirror and behold in it thine own mortality. Beg and pray to Christ that by the Easter festival thou mayest be awakened and come out of the labyrinth."

On the labyrinth in the Cathedral of Auxerre, the pelota ballgame or dance was performed annually on Easter Sunday in three-step rhythm, to the accompaniment of the rhythmic chant of the Easter antiphon. It was danced in a long chain along the labyrinth pattern by the dean or other church dignitary, and the canons. The ball or pelota, which the dean had received from the newly inducted canons, was handed down during the dance alternately, in wreathwise fashion along the line of dancers, who also revolved around his own axis. The essence of the dance was the circulation of the ball from the leader of the group to the other members and back from them to the leader, who was probably in the middle of the ring, robed in all his distinctive vestments. When the singing and dancing was over, the dean and chapter joined together in a sacred meal. The probable symbolism of the pelota dance is the representation of the apparent path or dance of the sun throughout the year, its "passion," and the corresponding passion of creation, analogous to the path of the incarnate Christ, his death, burial and resurrection as the Christ-Sun at Easter.[24]

From the middle of the twelfth century you find pictures of the Provencal May Day dance-song from Spain to Norway. It was particularly popular in Sweden, where it is first mentioned in 1260 as having been performed at a princely wedding, and there is a fresco of it in the Danish Cathedral of Orselev from about the year 1380. Numerous young Danes who were studying at the University of Paris saw it in the square before the Church of Our-Lady-of-the-Carole, and joined the dancers. The dance itself was a kind of processional. The dancers turned from right to left, in marching steps, beating one foot against the other. The choral-leader, or first-dancer, sported a glove, a nosegay or a flowery chaplet, a cup or May branch, or at night a torch, and led his company in a rapid advance.[25]

These folk dances which were included in the sacred worship continued to be a source of controversy within the Church. Some bishops, particularly in the northern European countries, spoke out against the paganism and tried to stop these kinds of celebrations. However, the clergy in Spain, Italy, and France tended to accept and incorporate the folk festival within the liturgy.

Another form of religious dance was to be found in certain Church festivals. These were particularly popular with the lower clergy, the monks, choirboys, younger priests, and subdeacons. Often they were highly disrespectful of the upper clergy. Just as was true in primitive religions, these festivals included various forms of acting, singing, dancing, and the playing of games.

John Beleth, who lived in the twelfth century and was the rector of the University of Paris, described four kinds of dance in use at Church festivals: the deacons' festival dance on St. Stephen's Day, the priests' on St. John's Day, the choirboys' on Innocents' Day, and the subdeacons' on the Feast of the Circumcision. It was the last of these which came to be known as the Festival or Feast of Fools. This was a New Year's celebration by the lower clergy which became a dramatic burlesque of the regular church service, with a caustic and licentious lampooning of the higher church dignitaries. From the end of the twelfth century on, the Feast of Fools spread throughout France and most of the other European countries. According to the records of Sens Cathedral, the festival typically included dancing, singing, drinking, and the parodying of religious offices, even those of the cardinal and pope.[26]

As described in a circular letter issued by the Theological Faculty of the University of Paris in 1444, the practices were "abominable"; priests and clergy who took part in it appeared in masks at divine service:

> ... or with distorted faces, or women's clothes, or dressed as bawds or actors, perform ring-dances, sing indecent songs, eat coarse bread, and play dice; leaping

and jumping they course through the church without shame.[27]

The letter of the faculty condemned these practices, and specifically forbade dancing, feasting, and drinking at the altar, and wearing masks or paint on one's face during the festival.

Other ceremonies which were of a dramatic or dance-like nature were carried on outside of the formal service of the church with a greater degree of approval by the authorities. A Children's Festival, or Festival of the Choristers, at which a child bishop was elected, was celebrated, usually on Innocents' Day, December 28. Elsewhere, ceremonies included various games, acting, singing, and feasting, without, however, the ridicule of the higher clergy or the regular service that made the Feast of Fools so objectionable.

There are many references to great processions which were carried on at this time with the approval of the clergy. Worshipers marched to ward off pain and distress or to bring relief from epidemics. They carried relics of saints and martyrs, crosses and banners, and images of the Holy Virgin. A source of the time says: "The relics were borne amidst happy dancing." The movement involved rhythmic steps, with the procession stopping at certain stations and performing sacral dances: ceremonial greetings, bows, turns, advancing, and retiring. One description of this ceremony describes it as:

> . . . a moving chorus advancing in harmony and with a sort of cadence through the various parts of the church. The processions passing through the choir and aisles, swinging the censer, do so to measured movements prescribed in the ritual . . . representing by their symbolic movements and figures holy and mystical dances.[28]

Within the mystical heritage of the Church there are various references to hymns and carols that suggest dance as an accepted liturgical art form. Found in the tenth century hymnary of the monastery of Moissac there is a hymn for morning Mass during the Easter festivals:

> His life, his speech and miracles,
> His wondrous death prove it.
> The congregation adorns the sanctity;
> Come and behold the host of ring dances.[29]

Another Church hymn sung during the Easter celebration includes references to the clapping of hands, singing, and dancing:

> The salvation of the earth is at hand;
> Ye mortals, clap your hands,
> Ye who are saved, sing
> Your songs of triumph!
> And with honest mind
> Before the Lord of the heavens.[30]

The following carol was sung during the eleventh century on the birthday of Mary:

> Now clap in applause,
> Ye men and women!
> Tune up in harmony
> Beautiful communal songs
> And dance ring dances
> In holy Mary's honor![31]

A century later we find these words in another hymn to Mary:

> I greet thee with garlands of roses;
> Ah! help us to the heavenly dance

And lead us to the wondrous light,
Which shines from the house of the saved.[32]

In a Spanish hymn to the virgin there are these lines:

Virgin, thou dost rise to everlasting triumph.
Thou dost rightly share the heavenly ring dance.[33]

The dean of Moosburg in Munich composed this song for a processional dance in 1360. It was sung by the priests and members of the congregation during the celebration of their ring dances.

This well-known, highly esteemed act
Brings again our bishop's blessing,
Dispersing as if in the light of dawn
The dark clouds of the depressed mind.

Chorus:
Therefore I free myself
From all sorrow that comes.

Numerous hands join and clasp in dance;
This broad and joyous path
Gives ample space for the chain of dancers.

Chorus:
Those who would be lured hence
To vicious habits are quickly stopped
And obey willingly and with joy
The church order.
All these festive gestures
Intend the gift of inward joy.[34]

These carols and hymns were sung and danced in stanza-chorus form. To carol means to dance. The division of some of these hymns and carols into a stanza and chorus shows us the shape the dance would have taken. During the stanza, which means stand or halt, the worshipers stood generally with their attention directed to the center of the circle and what was celebrated or believed. If it was a line carol, the focus would be on the destination of the dancers. During the repeated choruses the people would dance, using a three-step or tripudia. The tripudium was done both at a slow and medium speed, usually in an attitude of joy or jubilation. Jubilate is another translation for tripudia. The step can be traced to ancient Rome. The tripudium involved three steps forward and one step backward, and was used in ring dances, line dances, and processionals. It came to signify man's humility—"I go forward, yet I falter"—and was an act of reverence. It is the basis for genuflection still used in Christian worship.

During this early medieval period of Christian corporate worship, the priests and other holy dignitaries danced with the parishioners. Within the dances of the liturgy the movements of the individual soul were lost to the majestic rhythm of the Church. This dancing symbolized and suggested a sense of equality. During the eleventh and twelfth centuries the rising clerical hierarchy began an effort to separate themselves from the common people. Priests would only dance with other priests on certain days. Deacons would dance with deacons and the people were left to dance with themselves in holy worship. The bishops would sit alone, above everyone. Certain bishops, however, joined in the dancing of the people. This tended to threaten the authority of the Church and inadvertently led to the creation of new edicts and legislation against the use of dance in its various Christian forms.

The Later Medieval Period

In the later medieval period the same Church that had suppressed and denounced many forms of dance as pagan and degenerate now began to create its own dramatic portrayals. In an attempt to reach its parishioners and arouse public interest in the Church, it instituted more choral singing, picturesque processionals, and ceremonial dances performed in the choir area.

A forerunner to the mystery or miracle plays was the religious play as part of the Mass itself. These date from the early twelfth century. In a continuation of the Church's attempt to separate itself from the people, the plays were acted and danced by the clergy, holy sisters, and choirboys. One of the most enlightening is the Planctus from the Italian town of Cividale del Friuli. The actions and dance which accompany the lines and musical score are to be found initialed in color on the original fine vellum script:

Magdalene:
    O brothers!
    (Turns to the people with arms held out.)
    Where is my hope?
    (Beats her breast.)
    Where is my consolation?
    (Raises her hands.)

Where is my whole salvation,
(Inclines her head, casts herself at Christ's feet.)
O Master mine?

Mother:
    O sorrow!
    Deep sorrow!
    Why, why indeed,
    (Points to Christ with open hands.)
    Dear Son, hangest thou thus,
    Thou who art life
    (Beats her breast)
    And hast forever been?[35]

Then the disciple John speaks, and with his arms extended he points to Christ. He is followed by the Virgin Mary. Later both Mary Magdalene and the Virgin Mary speak together. The indications for movement of head and arms and of the whole body are similar in their stylized rigidity to Gothic art.

The veil worn by each Mary was either white or a liturgical color. Mary Magdalene's was often red. They generally carried boxes or painted vases for the spice and burial ointments. At the tomb door sat gilt angels crowned in white. They held candles or lamps and, to symbolize the resurrection, a palm or corn ear. The play was more chanted to music than spoken in a stage voice.

Mystery and miracle plays began to take form at this time. They were first presented within the church itself at the altar's east end, but soon they were moved out onto the broad west porches covered with colorful awnings picturing the saints. They were very popular with the people, and the cathedrals were packed to overflowing.

All kinds of purely secular ideas and incidents gradually crept in. Each biblical fact, bare enough in the Gospel, admitted not only a symbolic religious interpretation, but a human everyday significance as well, creating figures, which would have normally been remote and incomprehensible, into men as touching and familiar as one's neighbor, miller, clerk or farmer. French shepherds in leathern smocks would hail a cut-out gilded star hung from a beam and bear fresh vegetables or baby lambs to the crib of Christ. Melchior, Caspar and Balthasar, clad like kings of the Orient, brought more expensive toys, and King Herod would roar and stamp when the news comes of another king in Israel. Instead of being spoken in various accents of Latin which priests derived from Roman contacts, they spoke what we now call old English, old French or medieval German.[36]

The dancing which was included in these religious dramatizations was mainly theatrical and not devotional. However sacred their origins, these plays were shows, and it was not long before the ordained clergy was prohibited from participating in them.

The medieval world equated respectability with a certain kind of piety which demonstrated itself by the endowment of religious foundations. When the lords of the time died they gave the churches they possessed to the monasteries. As these monasteries grew and flourished, secular society began to look with a growing respect to the monks as the pick of the ecclesiastical population.

Many of the monastic orders during the twelfth and thirteenth centuries utilized dance to enhance the religious life of their disciplined groups. There are writings from various monks and friars of the period that illustrate these customs, such as the Cistercian Order's dances and prayers for the salvation of the universe, a treatise on dancing and its heavenly benefits by Friar Marti of Alicante, and lively celebrations of feast days with dances by the nuns of Villaceaux. The Franciscans were noted for their singing and dancing.

They called themselves the singing servants of Christ. A Franciscan monk, Fra Jacapone da Todi, wrote in 1270:

> Oh, that each one who loves the Lord would join in the dance, singing of his devotion.[37]

Another Franciscan, Bonaventura, writes of the redeemed singing songs of ceaseless praise:

> Blessed in soothe is that dance whose company is infinity, whose circling is eternity, whose song is bliss.[38]

A dance song, used for the ritual of the period in a monastery, that has been translated from the Latin reads as follows:

> Let the sober voice of the faithful sound,
> Turn round and round, O Sion, with joy;
> Let there be but one rejoicing of all
> Who have been redeemed by one only grace;
> Turn round and about, O Sion, with joy.[39]

The Dance of Death was the most widely known of all the religious dances from the twelfth to the sixteenth century. It was danced in Italy, Spain, France, Germany, and England. Much is to be learned about this dance from wall paintings and frescos. Interestingly there is no such representative art in Spain where it is generally believed that the dance originated.

There is much variety in these allegorical presentations of death displayed on the walls of churches, or on the borders of missals, where dancing skeletons lead partners from various walks of life. In the Cathedral of Salisbury Death addresses a single youth, while in the Alphabet of Holbein, and in the decorations of Jean Millot's Mors de la Pomme, a single figure of Death strikes down an individual in a group.

The earliest wall painting is Swiss, and was executed in 1312 at Klingenthal in Little Basel. The most famous are in the Charnel Cloisters of the Church of the Holy Innocents in Paris. There are included in these wall murals that illustrate the dance procession fifteen pairs of figures, each representing a different station in society ranging in descending order from Pope and emperor, to monk and knight, friar, peasant and child. The figures, both clerical and lay, speak in the inscriptions under the murals:

> Advance! See yourself in us, dead, naked, rotten and stinking. So will you be. . . .To live without thinking of this risks damnation. . . .The fattest rots first. . . .Power, honor, riches are naught; at the hour of death only good works count. . . .Everyone should think at least once a day of his loathsome end.[40]

Other medieval churchyards in Lubeck, Dresden, and Lucerne were decorated with similar frescos. There is a wall painting in the church Shakespeare knew in Stratford-on-Avon where perhaps these thoughts of Juliet's before she took the sleeping draught were born:

> Alack, alack, is it not like that I
> So early waking, what with loathsome smells
> And shrieks like mandrakes' torn out of the earth,
> That living mortals hearing them run mad:
> O, if I wake, shall I not be distraught,
> Environed with all these hideous fears,
> And madly play with my forefathers' joints?

Lincoln Kirstein suggests that there are three independent ideas in the Dance of Death. Before Death all men, whether they be great kings or poor laborers, are equal. In feudal Europe this equality, almost an idea of revenge on the rich, contributed enormously to the popularity of the parable. Secondly, there is the conception of living people confronted with their dead images, a development of a thirteenth-century French poem, "The Three Quick and the Three Dead." A trio of young nobles were hawking in a wood when they stumbled on three corpses who lectured them on human vanity. Finally there was the connection with actual miming and dancing.[42]

The Dance of Death sometimes followed a sermon by a Franciscan or Dominican priest emphasizing the terrors of death. The monk standing in a church or cemetery attempted to frighten the sinners into repentance. A figure or sometimes a group would come from the charnel house dressed in the traditional attire of Death—a close fitting yellowish suit painted to resemble a skeleton. Victims were enticed into dancing wildly with Death beyond the grave in whirling ecstasy.

One writer of the twelfth century, Giraldus Cambrensis, has left us in his *Itinerarium Cambriae* an exact description:

> You may see men or girls, now in the churchyard, now in the dance, which is led round the churchyard with a song, on a sudden falling on the ground as in a trance, then jumping up as in a frenzy, and representing with their hands and feet, before the people, whatever work they have unlawfully done on feast days; you may see one man put his hand to the plough, and another, as it were, goad on the oxen, mitigating their sense of labor, by the usual rude song: one man imitating the profession of a shoemaker; another, that of a tanner. Now you may see a girl with a distaff, drawing out the thread, and winding it again on the spindle; another walking, and arranging the threads for the web; another, as it were,

throwing the shuttle, and seeming to weave. On being brought into the church, and led up to the altar with their oblations, you will be astonished to see them suddenly awakened and coming to themselves.[43]

In the northern European countries, it was customary for these rites to include music. Backman suggests that the belief was that music exorcised the dead, forced them into compliance at being taken to the grave, and prevented them from walking the earth again; church bells were thought to drive demons away, and to comfort and protect the dead.[44]

That the dead liked to dance in the churchyards and cemeteries was a commonly held folk belief of the time. Death was thought to try to entice the living into the ranks of their ghostly dancing. There is within the Dance of Death the idea of the living themselves dancing toward their own death. According to the belief of the theologians of the time:

> The Dance of Death is actually a Dance of the Dead . . . in which the dead bodies lure the living from the various ranks of society in their midnight frolic. Later, the dead are conceived of no longer as corpses, but each as the personified figure of death himself.[45]

The Black Death, a combination of bubonic and pneumonic plague, ravaged Europe from 1347 to 1373. The effects varied from place to place. Holland almost completely escaped its toll, while elsewhere as much as half of the population died. The plague was felt most strongly in the towns and the monasteries. It was considered by most as a punishment from God. Death became a constant threat and was ever present. The peasants were particularly disadvantaged, for when the breadwinner died the serf's landlord took his best beast, and in many cases the priest took his second best. With most serfs owning only three cows it became a real

Flagellants in Bruges in 1349.
(Royal Library Brussels.)

Burial of victims of Black Death
at Tournel in Flanders in 1349.
(Royal Library Brussels.)

hardship for the remaining family. During the years of the plague when death was so very prevalent, men tried to drive out the devil by catching him. The Dance of Death was danced with hysteric gaiety and was often connected at this time with wakes for the dead.

With the occasional recurrence of the Black Death, Europe's population continued to drop. By the middle of the fifteenth century the rat-spread epidemic had destroyed more than half of Europe's inhabitants. The people's reaction to this startling diminution of their world, to the economic loss, and to the destruction of much of the ordinary life that they held dear can be seen in their ghoulish fascination with the vivid imagery of death. Nothing betrays more clearly the excessive fear of death felt in the Middle Ages than the preoccupation of the people with the Dance of Death.

As the Black Death continued to spread there was less improvising in the Dance of Death, and a set pattern began to evolve. These lines from a long poem written in 1480 show the kind of words Death spoke:

> O thow minstrel: that cannest so note and pipe
> Unto folkes: for to do plesaunce
> By the right honde anoon I shal the gripe
> With these others: to go up-on my daunce
> There is no scape: nowther a-voydaunce.

and the minstrel answers:

> This new daunce: is to me so strange
> Wonder dyuerse: and Parsyngli contrarie
> The dredful fotyng: doth so oft chaunge
> And the mesures: so ofte sithes varie
> Whiche now to me: is no thyng necessarie
> If hit were so: that I might asterte
> But many a man: if I shall not tarie
> Oft daunceth: but no thynge of herte.[46]

There was a Dance of Death game of Slavonic origin in which guests at a wake paired off to sing and dance. A sudden shrill note sounded, the music stopped, and in the silence everyone stood still. Then a sober sad melody started growing into a funeral dirge. One of the young men fell to the ground as if dead. The girls and women danced around him, circling the stricken youth with graceful mourning gestures. Then one after another they bent and knelt over the dead man, kissing him back to life. A joyful ring dance completed the first half of this game. The dance was then repeated with a young girl as the victim, and the mourners and dancers were all young men.

There was in Italy a spectacular representation of the Dance of Death in a macabre processional performed for the Duke of Florence. This magnificent pageant continued to be presented for over two hundred years. An account from 1507 reads:

The triumphal car was covered with black cloth, and was of vast size; it had skeletons and white crosses painted upon its surface, and was drawn by buffaloes, all of which were totally black: within the car stood the colossal figure of Death, bearing the scythe in his hand; while around him were covered tombs, which opened at all the places where the procession halted, while those who formed it chanted lugubrious songs, when certain figures stole forth, clothed in black cloth, on whose vestments the bones of a skeleton were depicted in white; the arms, breast, ribs and legs, namely, all which gleamed horribly forth on the black beneath. At certain distance appeared figures bearing torches, and wearing masks presenting the face of a death's head both before and behind; these heads of death as well as the skeleton necks beneath them, also exhibited to view, were not only painted with the utmost fidelity to nature, but had besides a frightful expression which was horrible to behold. At the sound of a wailing summons, sent forth with a hollow moan from trumpets of muffled yet inexorable clangor, the figures of the dead raised themselves half out of their tombs and, seating their skeleton forms thereon, they sang the following words, now so much extolled and admired, to music of the most plaintive and melancholy character. Before and after the car rode a train of the dead on horses, carefully selected from the most wretched and meager animals that could be found: the caparisons of those worn, half-dying beasts were black, covered with white crosses; each was conducted by four attendants, clothed in vestments of the grave; these last-mentioned figures, bearing black torches and a large black standard, were covered with crosses, bones and death's heads. While this train proceeded on its way, each sang, with a trembling voice, and all in dismal unison, that psalm of David called the Miserere.[47]

Dancing sometimes turned into an uncontrollable craze. There are numerous stories of this medieval dancing mania spreading all over Europe. According to one legend:

On Christmas night, 1013, a Parisian priest named Robert could not chant his Mass in peace, because he was bothered by the singing and dancing of carolers, eighteen young men and fifteen young girls who clamored in the cemetery outside. He told them to hush up and go away, but they only laughed at him and sang louder. So he cursed these bad Christians, saying, "May God make you all sing and dance the whole year through without missing one single day." And so it was they danced all night and all day, every day and every night. No one had seen such frenzy or such sadness, as they pounded the tombs of the dead. At the end of a year, Herbert, Bishop of Cologne, came to absolve them. As soon as the couples, joined together for twelve months, were permitted to separate, three of the girls, one of whom was the priest's daughter, fell down dead. The others slept for three days and three nights.[48]

The dancing mania was seen as a form of pathological aberration which was widely documented by writings of the thirteenth and fourteenth centuries. It affected both children and adults. In 1237, a large group of German children danced from Erfurt to Arnstadt, many dying along the way. A bridge at Marburg collapsed in 1278 beneath a horde of dancers and all drowned in the river below. In 1347 in spite of the efforts of many priests to stop them and break the spell that had seized them, several hundred men and women danced from Aix-la-Chapelle to Metz.

These outbursts represented some form of possession, equivalent perhaps to what Sachs had described as "convulsive dance" found among primitive tribesmen. They danced as if bewitched, and all the rites of exorcism that were tried failed to drive out the mysterious demons which had possessed them. Petrus de Herenthal, a fourteenth-century monk, described such dances carried on during the year 1374. There came to Aachen, he says, a curious sect of men and women from various regions of Germany:

Persons of both sexes were so tormented by the devil that in markets and churches, as well as in their own homes, they danced, held each other's hands and leaped high in the air. While they danced their minds were no longer clear, and they paid no heed to modesty though bystanders looked on. . . .They cried out names of demons . . . and that they were dying.[49]

The Church tried desperately to stop these dances and forbade them with many decrees. The Roman Synod ordered:

> In witness of the true and living God, the devilish songs which are heard at night on the graves of the dead are to cease, as well as the noise which accompanies them.

And a later resolution says:

> Whoever buries the dead should do so with fear, trembling and decency. No one shall be permitted to sing devil songs and perform games and dances which are inspired by the devil and have been invented by the heathen.[50]

The Chorisants, a sect believed by their contemporaries to be under diabolical influence, sprang up in Germany with a membership of men and women numbering in the thousands. The Nuremberg Chronicle in 1493 describes their actions:

> The people began to dance and rush about; they formed groups of three and danced in one place for half a day, and while dancing they fell to the ground and allowed others to trample on their bodies. By this they believed that they could cure themselves of illness. And they walked from one town to another and collected money from the people, wherever they could procure any. And this was carried on to such an extent that in the town of Cologne alone more than five hundred dancers were to be found. And it was a swindle, undertaken for the purpose of obtaining money, and that a number of them both men and women might be tempted to unchastity and succumb to it.

St. Vitus' Dance was another dance craze which spread over Europe from the eleventh to the fourteenth century. Here, men, women and children danced in wild delirium; they performed frenzied leaps and turns, writhing as if suffering from epileptic seizures, screaming out uncontrollably and foaming at the mouth. St. Vitus was invoked to cure the malady. According to tradition he had been responsible for curing the emperor's son of demonic possession. He became the patron saint of nervous diseases and his dance was considered of curative value. The name of St. Vitus became gradually connected with nervous disorders.

In Italy a similar mania was believed to be the result of the bite of a tarantula spider. Tarantism was eventually deliberately performed in order to avert the effects of the tarantula's poison. As the superstitious belief in this remedy diminished the dance continued in many provinces as the tarantella.

The medieval Church had been obliged to start from premises inherited from past generations during which the clergy had gradually adopted and consecrated popular beliefs into some of the most important Church ceremonies, holy days, and liturgical dances. Gregory the Great's advice to the missionaries who were sent to convert the English heathen is an example of this type of assimilation. He emphasized the necessity for compromise on unessential points:

> Let the old temples be baptized to the new Church uses;
> let heathen festivals be retained, but let them be diverted from the worship of devils to that of the true God.[51]

These compromises were undoubtedly wise and needed, yet they bore their inevitable fruit and together with pagan customs many pagan ideas sheltered themselves under the wing of the medieval Church.

Medieval thought was characterized by a struggle for unity. This passion for outward unity became one of the main concerns of the Church. Papal control was made more stringent over all aspects of Christian life. The excesses of the Dance of Death and the dancing manias which had swept all of Europe during the fourteenth century necessitated the Church's adoption of stronger regulations. Also, liturgical dance as it had been danced in worship up to this time was a great equalizer. The Church in its continued effort to establish a new strong leadership legislated more vigorously against it.

The priests, for unity's sake, were compelled to be all things to all men. The people were content to rally around the priest, for the Church with its strong sense of social solidarity gave them neighborly and religious warmth. Its ordinary ceremonies and dances and many of its beliefs, since they had sprung from the multitude, were therefore acceptable and comfortable to the multitude. It was the combination of this simple mystic religion among the people, the increased learning of the scholars, and the concurrent economic causes that set the stage for the change from the medieval to the Renaissance mind.

The Renaissance

Scholars now agree that the Renaissance or rebirth was basically a revolution in thought which began in Italy during the fourteenth century. As it spread throughout Europe, men looked for inspiration to the world of Greece and Rome. The questioning spirit of this new outlook gave rise to Protestantism and the Reformation, which plunged Europe into turmoil unparalleled since the adoption of Christianity. There continued a great diversity in the manner and uses of the dance in the Christian Church. Dante who is often credited with the beginnings of the Renaissance refers to Christian dancing in his *Divine Comedy*:

> Hosanna! Lord God of Sabaoth! . . . Thus, revolving to its own melody, that substance was seen by me to sing, and it and the others moved in their dance. . . . And as wheels within the fittings of clocks revolve, so that to him who gives heed the first seems quiet, and the last to fly, so these carols differently dancing, swift and slow, made me rate their riches.[52]

This view of the dance belonging to the movement of the angels is echoed by the painters of the Renaissance. Botticelli is noted for his angels dancing about the nativity scene. *Dance of the Angels* by Donatello also portrays angels

From Eve, being Adam's bride came sin,
Whence Death in turn did begin.
Then rage not, bride, should it befall
That death bites thee, as he bites all.
　　　　　　　—Hans Holbein

"The Bride," from Hans Holbein in *Dance of Death*, 1547.
(From the 1562 edition.)

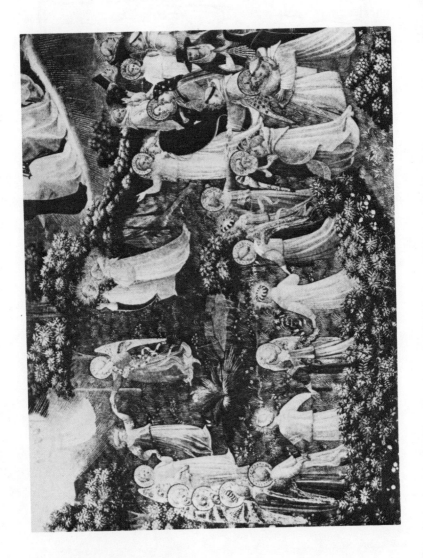

"Il Ballo dei Angeli," detail from
The Last Judgment by Fra Angelico
(Painting from Florence Academy.)

in symbolic movement. The artists of the Renaissance reveal the serenity and adoration expressed in much of the sacred dance of their time. Fra Angelico painted *The Last Judgment,* portraying a circular dance of saints and angels entering paradise. A poem of the time, "Il Ballo dei Angeli," describes the scene:

> Dance they in a ring in heaven
> All the blessed in that garden
> Where the love divine abideth
> Which is all aglow with love.
> In that ring dance all the blessed,
> In that ring dance all the angels.
> Go they before the Bridegroom,
> Dance, all of them for love.
> In that court is joyfulness
> Of a love that's fathomless.
> All of them go to the dancing
> For the Savior whom they love.[53]

Books began to be printed after 1455. Printing made the spread of literacy much easier and Europe a community subject to common ideas. The power to read and write is an instrument of authority if it belongs to a few but a stepping stone to equality if it belongs to many. Both governments and the Church tried in accordance with their traditions to keep their own control over man's mind.

The movement of change in the Renaissance was gradual. The new emerging technology was still primitive. Travel and transport were slow and continued to insure a society that was often provincial. There was much of the fifteenth century that was medieval at heart. Many local and regional peculiarities continued to exist.

In England there was still much pressure against the dancing and levity of the pilgrims. In 1407, Archbishop

Arundel, in his interrogation of William Thorpe, voiced some of the complaints:

> Finding out one pilgrimage, they will ordain with them beforehand to have with them both men and women that can well sing wanton songs; and some other pilgrims will have with them bagpipes: so that every town they come through, what with the noise of their singing, and with the sound of their piping, and with the jangling of their Canterbury bells, and with the barking out of dogs after them, they make more noise than if the King came there away, with all his clarions and many other minstrels.

But the representative of the Church defended the merriment in vigorous words:

> Lewd! Loose! Thou seest not far enough in this matter! For thou considerest not the great travail of pilgrims. . . . I say to thee that it is right well done that pilgrims have with them both singers and also pipers: that when one of them that goeth barefoot striketh his toe upon a stone, and hurteth him sore and maketh him to bleed; it is well done, that he or his fellow, begin then a song or else take out of his bosom a bagpipe to drive away with much mirth the hurt of this fellow.[54]

The Church of the fifteenth century was caught in a tangle of cross-current and similar expression with both minstrel and folk dance. The Church used and imitated the court's celebrations with elaborate processionals and dramatic presentations. Allegorical masques were used in symbolic dancing to heighten the dramatic mood. One such religious and social entertainment was presented in 1462 by King René of Provence on the eve of Corpus Christi. It was without a single plot, rather portraying separate dramatic episodes: the Roman gods Mars and Minerva, Pan, Pluto, and Proserpine, King Herod persecuted by devils, ancient Jews dancing around a golden calf, Christ and the apostles, Death with a scythe, and the magi following a star. The Corpus Christi processions were representative of the many religious dances of the period that were both entertaining and devotional in nature.

In these sorts of dances the appearance of the dance became more important than its inward satisfaction to the dancer. The original use of the dance in Christianity to externalize internally felt ideas and emotions had begun to wane. Guglielmo Ebreo, a religious leader of 1480, explains the benefits of the sacred dance. This description is one which is in keeping with the understanding of the nature of Christian dance as expressed by Rudolph Laban and other contemporary movement experts.

> Dancing is an action showing outwardly the spiritual movements which must agree with those measures and perfect concords of harmony which, through our hearing and with earthly joy, descend into one's intellect, there to produce sweet movements which, being thus imprisoned, as it were, in defiance of nature, endeavor to escape and reveal themselves through movement. The art of dancing is for generous hearts that love it. It is a matter entirely different from and mortally inimical ... to the depraved minds which turn it from a liberal art and virtuous science into a vile, adulterous affair.[55]

The Reformation, which began in 1525, eventually put an end to dance within the service of the Church. There are many factors which led to the Reformation. Some resented the restrictions placed on Bible reading, and the educated people disliked the superstitions connected with pilgrimages and indulgences. Many of the dances that had evolved from pagan origins also met heavy criticism. The intellect began to be the most important sense of the body. Ironically, Martin Luther, the Reformation instigator himself, did not hold these negative views of the dance. He wrote in 1540:

> I always loved music; whoso hath skill in this art, the same is of good kind and fitted to all things. Dances have been instituted and permitted in order that courtesy may be learned in company and to encourage friendship and acquaintance among young men and girls.[56]

In "From Heaven High," a carol which Martin Luther wrote, there are these stanzas which reflect his love of children and their natural way of expressing joy with singing, skipping, and dancing.

> A little child for you this morn
> Has from a chosen maid been born,
> A little child so tender, sweet,
> That you should skip upon your feet.
>
> I can play the whole day long.
> I'll dance and sing for you a song,
> A soft and soothing lullaby
> So sweet that you will never cry.[57]

William Tyndale, another early Protestant church leader, in his Prologue to the New Testament uses these words to describe the joy of the good news:

> That we cal gospel is a greke word, and signyfyth good, mery, glad and joyfull tydings, that maketh a mannes hert glad, and maketh hym synge, daunce, and leepe for ioye.[58]

The ensuing leaders of the Reformation were not as kindly disposed to dancing as its founder. Protestant clergy quickly took up a grim tone toward dancing. Melchior Ambach, a Frankfort preacher, said it was sinful because it was not founded on the Bible. Most church irritation however, was political and directed against the balls of the nobility.

The Counter-Reformation tried to reform the Church from within and to fight the spread of Protestantism. This commitment to internal reform necessitated a close look at all the traditions of the Church. The Council of Trent was set up in 1545 to try to sort out the religious confusion felt by the people. The Council did little more than turn the head of the Church against Protestantism. The dance generally continued much as before, and it was still encouraged in some places such as Spain.

The pavane, with its characteristics of a somber religious mood, originated in the formal and austere court life of Inquisitional Spain. Dancing continued as an integral part of the ceremony in the churches of Spain. This close relationship to the Church gave music much of its chant-like quality. The pavane *Saint Thomas' Wake* by John Bull suggests a religious conception. Thoinot Arbeau, a Spanish authority of the sixteenth century, refers to the pavane:

> Our musicians play it when a damsel of good family is taken to Holy Church to be married, or when musicians head a religious procession of the chaplains, masters, and brethren of some notable guild.[59]

The first ballet presented in 1581 by Catherine de Medici at Fontainebleau was entitled *Ballet Comique de la Reine*. It was a mixture of Old Testament tales and Greek and Roman mythology. The dance had finally left the Church after years of being a form of religious expression for the people. Thousands viewed the spectacle of this first ballet, but did not dance themselves.

As late as the sixteenth century some clergy still continued to encourage dance within the liturgy. In 1588, Arbeau wrote a strong defense of religious dancing:

> For one who has spoken ill of dances, there are an infinity of others who have praised and esteemed them. The holy and royal prophet David danced before the ark of the Lord. And as for the holy prophet Moses, he was not angered to witness dancing, but grieved because it was performed round a golden calf, which was idolatry. In the early Church there was a custom which has endured until our time to sing the hymns of our faith while dancing, and this may still be observed in some places. We practice such merry-making on days of wedding celebrations, and of the solemnities of the feasts of our Church, even though the reformers abhor such things; but in this matter they deserve to be treated like some hind-quarter of goat put into dough without lard.[60]

Although dancing has not remained as a part of oratorios, it was originally included. The oratorio *La Rappresentazione di Anima e di Corpo* by Emilio de Cevalieri was performed in the oratory of the Chiesa S. Maria in Vallicella in Rome in 1600. The following stage directions show how the original oratorio is made varied and dramatic through symbolic dances:

> The verse beginning Chiostri altissimi estellati must be sung accompanied by stately and reverent steps. To these will succeed other grave steps and figures of a solemn character. During the ritornelli the four principal dancers will perform a ballet embellished with capers

without singing. And thus, after each verse, the steps of
the dance will always be varied, the four chief dancers
sometimes using the gagliarde, sometimes the cenario,
and sometimes the corrente which will do well in the ri-
tornelli.[61]

Dances continued to be used by the churches for festivals and holidays. An Easter dance was performed annually
in the churches of the diocese of Besancon. Included in the
book of rites of the Church of St. Marie Magdaleine from
1582, we find the following description:

> The canons held hands in a ring; behind them was a sec-
> ond ring composed of choirboys, each paired with a can-
> on, while in the center was the chief dignitary, the senior
> in rank with the smallest chorister in attendance. After
> this, the circle broke up, and the oldest and youngest led
> the way in a serpentine or labyrinthine dance.[62]

During the Renaissance, all special occasions included
some form of dance, whether they were dance-dramas,
dances at funerals or weddings, or dances of a religious nature. Sir John Davies illustrates this in his poem of 1594,
"Orchestra":

> Since when all ceremonious mysteries,
> All sacred orgies and religious rights,
> All pomps, and triumphs, and solemnities,
> All funerals, nuptials, and like publike sights,
> All parliaments of peace, and warlike fights,
> All learned arts, and every great affaire
> A lively shape of Dauncing seemes to beare.
>
> Thus they who first did found a common-weale,
> And they who first Religion did ordaine
> By dauncing first the peoples hearts did steale,

Of whome we now a thousand tales doe faine,
Yet doe we now their perfect rules retaine,
And use them still in such devices new
As in the world long since their withering grew.

As the Renaissance drew to a close the sacred dance continued. Johannes Boemus tells of Christmas Eve dances in the churches of old Franconia in 1620:

With what rejoicing did not only the priest, but also the people, celebrate in the churches the birth of Christ. . . . They placed on the altar a doll representing the Christ child, after which the boys and girls hopped a ring dance around the altar.[63]

Raffaello delle Colombe, a Dominican monk, said in 1622:

The dance is a symbol of the universal order and can be compared with the dance of the stars. For prayer is a spiritual dance. . . . God leads the ring dance of the heavenly bodies. God leads inside the ring.[64]

In 1682, Father Menestrier, a Jesuit priest from Paris, definitely attached dance to the ritual of sacred service:

The divine office was made up of psalms, hymns, and canticles, for the praises of God were recited, sung, and danced. . . . The place where these religious acts were performed in divine worship was called the choir, just as with the choroi of the Greeks. In Latin, the prelates were called praesules . . . for in the choir, at the divine office, they played the same part as the leader of the dances.[65]

During the Renaissance the dance in Christianity flourished in the theatrical allegorical ballets, in processional celebrations, in the oratorio, and in the interpretation of hymns and psalms in worship. The Church itself put a stop to these acts of worship in the post-Renaissance period. Neither the Roman Catholic Church nor the Protestant Christian Churches would allow sacred dances in their services. There were a variety of reasons for their decisions. Although they themselves had used it, they did not approve of the theatrical use of the dance. They found the folk acceptance of the dance to be pagan and without credence. With the printing of tracts, pamphlets, and books the mind became all important and the body was thought to be useless to religious growth. But, according to Backman, it was the Reformation itself with its highly critical attitude toward the traditional Church customs and its fight against images, the worship of saints and pilgrimages that ultimately succeeded in suppressing the Church dance.

Post-Renaissance

Although the Reformation is credited with putting an end to the dance in Christianity as it had been known up to that point, several of the new denominations and sects which were outgrowths from it continued to use dance within their worship.

In Colonial America dancing was not in as much disfavor with the Puritans, as so often has been thought. In his book about the Puritans and music and dance in New England, Percy Scholes illustrates many instances of its acceptance with the colonists. Dancing, however, was thought to be pagan when it was associated with feasts or public demonstrations. When dancing was used as it had been in the Bible it was not wrong and was accepted.

John Cotton the leading minister of Boston, expressed how ministers felt about dancing:

> Dancin, yea though mixt, I would not simply condem. For I see two sorts of mixt dancings in use with God's people in the Old Testement, the one religious, Exod. XV, 20, 21, and other civil, tending to the praise of conquerors, as the former of God, I Samuel XVII, 6, 7. Only lascivious dancing to wanton ditties, and amorous gestures and wanton dalliances, especially after feasts, I would bear witness against, as a great flabella libidinis.[66]

Increase Mather, the father of Cotton Mather, wrote the tract *Against Profane and Promiscuous Dancing: Drawn Out of the Quiver of the Scriptures, By the Ministers of Christ at Boston in New England.* As the title itself suggests Rev. Mather admits the biblical base for dancing and was only against dancing that aroused the passions:

> Concerning the Controversy about Dancing, the question is not whether all Dancing be in itself sinful. It is granted, that Pyrrhical or Polemical Saltation: i.e. where men vault in their Armour, to shew their strength and activity, may be of use. Nor is the question, whether a sober and grave Dancing of Men with Men, or of Women with Women, be not allowable; we make no doubt of that, where it may be done without offence, in due season, and with moderation. The Prince of Philosophers has observed truly, that Dancing or Leaping is a natural expression of joy: so that there is no more Sin in it, than in laughter, or any outward expression of inward Rejoycing.[67]

Cotton Mather in 1703 expressed the continuing thought about dance within worship. There is contained within this statement, "The Magnalia Christi Americana," arguments which serve to illustrate the gathering confusion:

> The Instrumental Music used in the old Church of Israel was an institution of God; it was the commandment of the Lord by the Prophets; and the Instruments of the Lord. Now there is not one word of Institution in the New Testament for Instrumental Music in the Worship of God. And because the holy God rejects all he does not command in his worship, he now therefore in effect says to us, I will not hear the melody of thy Organs. But, on the other hand, the rule given doth abundantly inti-

mate that no voice is now heard in the Church but what is significant, and edifying by signification, which the voice of Instruments is not.

Though Instrumental Music were admitted and appointed in the worship of God under the Old Testament, yet we do not find it practiced in the Synagogue of the Jews but only in the Temple. It thence appears to have been a part of the ceremonial Pedagogy which is now abolished; nor can any say it was a part of moral worship. And whereas the common usage now hath confined Instrumental Music to Cathedrals, it seems therein too much to Judaize, which to do is a part of the Anti-Christian Apostasy, as well as to Paganize. If we admit Instrumental Music in the worship of God, how can we resist the imposition of all the instruments used among the ancient Jews? Yea, Dancing as well as playing, and several other Judaic actions?[68]

By the end of the eighteenth century, religious dances in the new world were scarce and scattered with the exception of a new group that joined dancing and religion. The Shakers were a unique sect that created intricate religious dances. They came to America in 1774 descending from a group called the United Society of Believers in Christ's Second Appearance from Manchester and Bolton, England. The Shakers traced their spiritual lineage to the ancient tradition for dancing as part of the adoration of God. Their beliefs came from the Albigenses, a thirteenth-century group whose members had used dance as a way of adoration.

The term Shaker came from the rapid up and down movement of the hands with the action mostly in the wrists. When the participants shook their hands with the palms turned down toward the floor, the symbolic motion meant that they were shaking out "all that is carnal." When the palms were turned upward as if to receive spiritual blessing, the quick up and down, shaking movement expressed the open petition "Come, life eternal." Aside from this common motion of the hands, there were many pantomimed gestures to interpret their songs. General movements included bowing, bending, and a great deal of turning, for the latter motion symbolized turning away from evil and around toward God and good:

> I'll turn, turn, turn, turn, away from all evil,
> And come, come, come, come, into the gospel.[69]

The small group of Shakers who came to America settled in Niskeyuna, near Albany, New York. They had an extremely strict code, founding a religious order that was separate from the world, rejected a corrupt society, and foreswore marriage and all carnal practices. The sect grew rapidly after the Revolution and spread throughout the east and midwest. It increased to about six thousand followers in 1850.

The behavior at their early prayer meetings resembled the dance mania of the Middle Ages. A meeting in 1780 was described thus:

> Everyone acts for himself, and almost everyone different from the other; one will stand with his arms extended ... another will be dancing, and sometimes hopping on one leg around the floor; another will fall to turning around ... another will be prostrate on the floor ... some trembling extremely, others acting as though all their nerves were convulsed.[70]

Gradually, the dancing which had been based on individualized expression changed to a more ordered and structured form, including the square-order shuffle which was

patterned on the vision of angels dancing around the Throne
of God. Men and women moved in separate groups with
shuffling steps, advancing and retreating. Their hands and
bodies vibrated as they danced forward and back, turned and
bent in supplication, or lifted their heads high in ecstasy. The
Shakers developed more complex formations, in circles, lines
and weaving patterns. The dances revealed a new symbolic
meaning:

> The devotees felt that they were indeed marching heav-
> enward, that the circle was the perfect emblem of their
> union. The "wheel-within-a-wheel, three or more con-
> centric circles turning in alternate directions around a
> central chorus, became a figure of the all-inclusiveness of
> their gospel; the outer ring the ultimate circle of truth,
> the Shaker dispensation; the singers, the harmony and
> perfection of God that were at the heart of life. In an-
> other exercise, "The Narrow Path," a single file of danc-
> ers, with heads bowed, placed one foot before the other
> as they trod the narrow way to salvation.[71]

The beauty of the rhythmic movements of the Shakers
is described by the artist Benson Lassing in 1850:

> The movements in the dance or march whether natural
> or studied are all graceful and appropriate; and as I
> gazed upon that congregation of four or five hundred
> worshipers marching and countermarching in perfect
> time, I felt that . . . the involuntary exclamation of even
> the hypercritical would be, "How beautiful!"[72]

Walt Whitman after seeing a Shaker circle dance which
symbolized Ezekiel's wheel said:

> The singing in the center represented the harmony and
> perfection to which all tend, and there is God.[73]

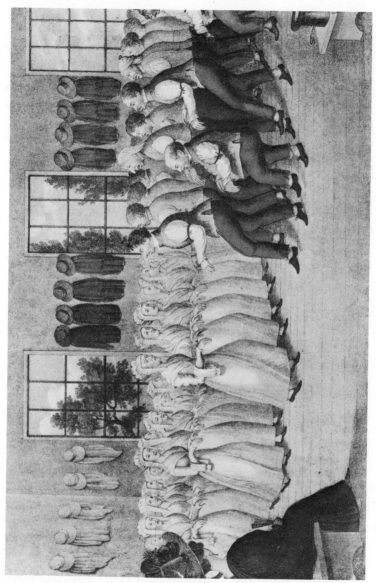

Shakers near Lebanon, Lithograph by N. Currier.
(The Harry Peters Collection, Museum of the City of New York.)

"The Dance of Death" by Jacob von Wyl.
The abbott and abbess are called by death.

Gradually, the Shaker communities that had flourished began to decline. The Shakers followed an early ruling of the religious group that there should be no marrying among believers. They expected the second coming of Christ, as the first-century Christians had. As a result of these beliefs their lack of growth is readily understandable. With the virtual end of the Shaker movement in the late nineteenth century, the dance of the people in worship ended.

The dance had been a part of Christianity since its beginnings as illustrated by this entry in the first edition of the *Encyclopaedia Britannica* of 1768:

> Dance, an agreeable motion of the body, adjusted by art to the measures or tune of instruments, or of the voice. Dancing is usually an effect and indication of joy. It has been in use among all nations, civilised and barbarous and sometimes made an act of religion. The Christians are not free from this superstition; for in popish countries certain festivals, particularly those of the Sacrament and passion of our Lord, are celebrated with dancing.[74]

Church dances had always been comparatively numerous until the seventeenth century. Actually, there had never been a period when there was no dance associated with the Latin religious system. Dance had served, as we have seen, several distinct functions. Inside the church it served as a basic part of the liturgy or as a portion of a periodic ceremony such as a baptism or holy day, and in the mystery or miracle plays often used to spread doctrine. Outside the church the primary occasion was usually the initial dedication and opening of the building for religious use, often culminating in another processional ritual dance inside the church. The funeral, burial and graveyard memorial dances were also done outside the church. There were many professional dances, from some gathering place such as the fields or harvest center, where the people danced toward and into the church. Also, there were always the unsanctioned popular memorial dances of the people both inside the church and in the churchyard.

It is difficult to discern changes which are actually made through generations. Continuities are never wholly broken, but eventually much of the movement of the people in worship was assumed by the priest, and the Mass itself came to be seen in the Roman Catholic Church as dance. The Mass was described as dance by Ralph Adams Cram, a Boston theologian, in 1897:

> It is thus beside the point whether one calls the ministers' role in the liturgy acting or dancing. Unless they are saints they will not come to the altar full of "solemnity and awe," and if they are to invoke within themselves what it is their duty to invoke in everyone else, the ministers and their attendants must act, dance, or whatever. The sacred dance, like all liturgical art, must struggle for the incarnation in it of the supernatural if it is to be transfigured. In the Holy Place, at the heart of the liturgy, it can most easily be debased.[75]

In his book, *The Mass in Slow Motion,* Ronald Knox refers to the Mass as a ritual dance which has lasted throughout the centuries of the Christian Church:

> The introit gives you a nice sense of squaring your shoulders.... After the introit we go on to the real grovel. The point is that whenever you approach almighty God in prayer you ought to be bowled over, at the very start, by the thought of his unutterable greatness.... So, we say Kyrie eleison.... And the thing we use to cheer us up is the Gloria in excelsis.... And when, at the beginning of the Gloria, the priest parts his

hands and raises them and then brings them together again with that sort of scooping motion, he is as it were inviting our Lord to become incarnate and come down to earth. In saying, "The Lord be with you," the priest puts his hands apart, and then brings them together again. . . . I think there's an obvious . . . significance about this latest movement in the dance. The priest, as he swirls around to make us feel at home, wants to include all of us in his greeting, and so he stretches his hands out wide. . . . All through this bit, the movements of the dance are rather complicated. You have come to Mass to worship God, and that means worshiping God with your whole being, not just bits of it. Oremus generally means something is going to happen; a new movement in the dance is just going to begin. The Mass is a continuous action. The offertory is really rather an important part of the Mass, and all the more so because, in a sense, this is where you come on. . . . Those two small boys in red cassocks . . . represent the congregation. In theory, you are all crowding into the sanctuary, turning the priest's solitary dance into a tumultuous round dance. The Mass is like that; we alternate continually between rushing to God with the consciousness of our needs, and then being driven back into a kind of shame-faced, tongue-tied humility by the thought of God's majesty and our insignificance. Those are the two motifs that constantly cross and recross, making up the pattern of the dance for us. We unite, in offering the Mass, not only with all faithful Christians all over the world, but with the dead too. With these, the pure in heart, we will form one single ring about the eternal altar. Sursum corda; lift up your hearts! It means to take a deep breath and let your whole self go out to God in the spirit of gratitude—the characteristic attitude of Christian people in worshiping their God in thankfulness. Don't encourage the choir to make the Sanctus into a great hullabaloo. The whole dance of the Mass depends, just here, on getting that effect of sudden calm, sudden dying away of noise. It's as if the priest says, "Sssh! I've seen it—the glory of God that fills earth and heaven, shining in front of me. Take off your shoes, and let's go in very quietly, on tiptoe." I have represented the Mass to you as a kind of ritual dance.[76]

The dance in Christianity is barely recognizable today. It is submerged in the symbolic movements of the clergy, whether it be the Mass itself or the minister's raised arms and upturned palms in the benediction. The dance of the people is seen in the kneeling of the celebrants at the communion rail, the genuflection upon entering the presence of the Lord, the bowed head in prayer, and the hands held firmly together in a gesture of supplication. These then are the remnants of a glorious past—a past that had the potential of leaving us with a liturgy of sacred dance which could have compared with our vast heritage of sacred music, a legacy of Christian dance which has not yet materialized. There would be dance choirs and various other dance experiences in the future, but the regular or usual use of dance as a participatory part of the liturgy of the Christian Church had ended.

The Twentieth Century

Historically as worship became more cerebral it took very seriously the importance of words in communicating and responding to the Gospel. The Church in the years following the Reformation did not acknowledge the fact that our humanity is not just a matter of disembodied intellects. Our humanity includes our physical bodies, too, and we are capable of using more to communicate with God than just our ears and mouth. The Church of the twentieth century has begun to realize that we can praise God with our whole bodies. Worship involves our whole being and not just our mind. The importance of the body as a vehicle of communication has started to be understood. There has been an increasing interest in reviving old and adding new expressions of worship to the liturgy.

The earliest innovator in the field of religious dance was Ruth St. Denis who began experimenting in 1912. She was soon joined by Ted Shawn, and together they formed the Denishawn School. The first dancing in this century in Protestant Christian worship was presented by them in 1917 at the Interdenominational Church in San Francisco. The opening prayer, the doxology, a Gloria, an anthem, the twenty-third psalm and the sermon "Ye Shall Know the Truth" were all danced. It was an auspicious beginning and was well received by the critics and large congregation.

During the following years St. Denis and Shawn toured the country with the "Dance Church Service" and other dance programs such as his "Jesu, Joy of Man's Desiring" and "Oh Brother Sun" and her well-known "The Masque of Mary." They danced in cathedrals, churches, halls and theatres, and were responsible for inspiring and training dancers, religious groups, and church leaders wherever they went. In 1964, on the fiftieth anniversary of work in their profession, they were recognized in an article in *Time* magazine for their contribution to the growth of religious dance.

Other leaders of the dance soon followed. Among the most notable was Erika Thimey of Washington, D.C. who was responsible for many religious dances in mainly Unitarian churches in Chicago, New York, and Boston in the mid-1930's. Margaret Fisk Taylor has become one of the best-known proponents of Christian dance. She directed rhythmic choirs in Hanover, New Hampshire from 1938 until 1950. Since that time her efforts have been devoted to teaching in seminaries, leading workshops, and writing books about the uses of dance in worship.

As the number of dance choirs gradually grew the leaders of the various groups felt a need to come together to exchange ideas that would help promote the dance. They met informally in New England as the Eastern Regional Sacred Dance Association for three years. The Sacred Dance Guild was a natural outgrowth of this organization and was officially organized in 1958. The membership includes all denominations and is made up of over four hundred men and women who are both students of the dance and dance choir directors. The guild continues to grow and serve as a source of information for dancers and persons interested in the use of dance in worship as a religious expression.

In more recent years, modern communication media

"The Passion According to Mary"
Carla De Sola and Greg Reynolds.
(Photo by Ginerva Portlock.)

Carlos Carvajal's "Totentanz" at Grace Cathedral, San Francisco.)
(Photo by Leonard J. Cosky.)

have made us more conscious of the non-verbal. Television in particular concentrates on action. Words remain as a basic form of communication, but the new electronic media take us one step further, showing the actions that words describe. Words are less important. They no longer monopolize communication except in much of Christian worship.

Marshall McLuhan, the communications theorist, insisted that modern man is post-literate—that he has gone beyond the medium of the printed page as his prime means of communicating information, after five hundred years of the Gutenberg age. He believed that modern man has acquired perceptual patterns resembling those of pre-literate man, and that they are both stimulated by the visual, by action, and by the sense of touch to a greater degree than literate man. A renewed stress on non-verbal forms, characteristic of early Christian worship, again makes sense to modern man. The Christian Church may well move into the future by recovering some of the forms of worship used in the past which can better communicate with post-literate people.

There are many places in the United States today where dance is regaining its original function as part of Christian worship. The west coast has Carlos Carvajal in San Francisco who has become known for his "Totentanz." In New York there is Carla DeSola and her Omega Liturgical Dance Company, and in the hills of Vermont the Benedictine Monks dance in worship as part of their liturgy.

Carlos Carvajal's "Totentanz" is a spell-binding five-part dance pageant that recreates the diverse elements of the Dance of Death and dancing manias so prevalent in the Middle Ages. It was created for his M.A. thesis at Stanford University and was first presented by the San Francisco Ballet in 1967. Since that time it has usually been danced by his company Dance Spectrum at Grace Cathedral where the architecture and atmosphere of the building add to the essence of the dance. You are artfully transported back in time and place to the medieval years of the dance's origin.

The inevitability of death is constantly felt in the work from its first scene, "Carrying Out King Carnival," where the children's games "Blind Man's Bluff" and "Ring Around the Rosy" are interrupted by the Pied Piper leading them to a felt doom. Superstitions of the era abound in the cheerful games: the blind man in "Blind Man's Bluff" was death; the verse, "Ashes, ashes, we all fall down," refers to the burning of contaminated buildings. "Ring around the Rosy" was the red swelling encircling the mouth which was an initial sign of the plague.

The second scene, "Processional at Verges," finds flagellants, pilgrims, and other traditional characters of death carrying out the ancient spectacle of a village procession in Catalonia.

In the following scene, "Murals at Basel," the art of the period is brought to life as the dialogue between death and the wall murals is danced.

The fourth scene, "Death's Pawn," shows the hypnotic state of the time as the Pawn seduces the dancers in a manner of persistent intervention into killing each other.

The dance ends with "Dies Irae" in which "all of us" are literally felt to be drawn into the dance mania and swept up by death in whirling ecstasy.

"Totentanz" is presented in a manner and style reminiscent of the dance spectacles and allegorical dramas of the Church of the Renaissance. The content of the dance is a comprehensive and complete representation of the varying forms of the Dance of Death during the medieval period that evokes an understanding not possible by merely reading about the age.

Carlos Carvajal's works are mainly presented in

churches on the west coast. He seldom works with non-professionals. His outstanding contributions to Christian dance have been in the area of education and enlightenment as he has simultaneously introduced both the experience and history of the dance in Christianity.

On the east coast there is Carla DeSola who is in residence with her Omega Liturgical Dance Company at the Cathedral Church of St. John the Divine. Carla who founded the group in 1974 works unceasingly to open the world of Christian dance to a growing number of people. This Juilliard graduate who studied with Jose Limon and Valeria Bettis has danced in churches, universities, and retreat centers. In the past year she and her Omega Company have performed at the fiftieth anniversary celebration of the Jesuit Spiritual Center in Wernersville, Pennsylvania, Temple Emanuel in Yonkers, New York, where they danced "Hassidic Suite," a celebration service for the Reformed Church in America at Warwick, New York, a teaching conference at the Pacific School of Religion in Berkeley, California, and a festival of religious arts at the First English Lutheran Church in Baltimore, Maryland.

One of the most moving of the Omega Liturgical Dance Company's offerings is "The Passion According to Mary," a dance drama based on the passion of Christ from the point of view of his mother. It is about the loss of a child as seen through his mother's eyes. "Passion" in this sense means the pain, anguish and despair expressed by Mary. It was choreographed and set to parts of Bach's "St. Matthew Passion" by Greg Reynolds, the group's associate choreographer. He and Carla danced it as part of the liturgy at the General Convention of the Episcopal Church in Denver, Colorado.

Carla DeSola has received the respect and admiration of all faiths. Her effort is divided between performances and teaching, with approximately half of her time devoted to instructing other people and then allowing them to participate in the fullness of the dance experience. It is her work with children, however, that may ultimately prove to be her most important.

She is teaching Christian dance to the students at the Cathedral School of St. John the Divine. In a recent spring dance which celebrated the new birth of earth, the children entered in brightly colored leotards, observed the earth and danced in gentle joy. The grass grew with light movement. They did cartwheels and saw the earth upside down. The youngsters became dizzy and rolled into cocoons, reappearing as bright butterflies. They bent and picked up colorful streamers and in a circular spiral softly whirled, expressing the many hues and essences of this earth. The young worshipers were enthralled and responded to their classmates. As the children she teaches continue to grow, learning about dance and using it in their worship, Christian dance will become more firmly rooted in the future.

DeSola's work is a combination of teaching, dance presentation and actual parts of the liturgy danced as they would have been within the early Church. The Omega Company has become one of the best known liturgical dance companies in the country, but it is not unique. It is representative of many groups across our nation who are endeavoring to reawaken an interest and delight in the use of the dance in Christianity.

In the sturdy Green Mountains of Vermont, the Benedictine Monks of Weston Priory worship with joyful dance. This small religious community was started in 1953 by Brother Leo, who at that time was Abbot of Dormition Abbey in Jerusalem. Its traditions and rule reach back through the centuries-old succession of monasteries deriving from Benedict's original community.

The priory in Weston became locally autonomous in 1968. It is involved with the rhythm of the seasons, cultivat-

"St. Benedict's Dance" the Benedictine Monks of Weston, Vermont.
(Weston Priory Photo.)

Worshipping in a festive dance during a service at Weston Priory, Vermont.
(Weston Priory Photo.)

ing both agriculturally and spiritually. In the pastoral setting each brother's individual gifts are supported and encouraged as they adhere to St. Benedict's teachings and actively seek to discern the fruits of the Holy Spirit. Each monk's talents are called forth and utilized on behalf of the community. They are able to be free to create and be for others.

Prayer is at the center of their common life. They meet together four times a day for worship. Music and dance are special gifts which are evident at these times of gathering. The dance typifies the happiness and spirit of the community. It is understandable not only to the brothers but also to the guests who often join them in their worship. The celebration of the Eucharist is most often a time for dance. They also dance when they want to come together with joy and at times when words seem insufficient and unable to express their feelings and emotions. Sometimes Scripture is used to set the context, and a dance will follow to amplify and explain.

Brother Leo's hope had been to establish a community where there was an equality between the brothers and the priests. He saw it as a fertile seedbed open to the Holy Spirit. The dance at Weston Priory has been a great equalizer and leveler; it is seen by the brothers as helpful in their attainment of the spirit of monastic tradition.

The dances that the monks do are simple church dances. "Heve Ma Tov" based on Psalm 132 and "Ma Navu" from Isaiah are Hebrew dances that Jesus might have danced. They do Greek and Yugoslavian dances set to original music written by Brother Gregory. One of their favorite and most moving dances is a Shaker dance, "It's A Gift To Be Simple, It's A Gift To Be Me."

The Benedictine Monks at Weston Priory use the dance in worship because it is not complicated. They use it to help make their intent more accessible. It brings them together in a oneness of spirit and joy. The dance at Weston is more nearly the dance of the early Church. It is never performed but is done by the worshiper in worship. An integral and important part of the liturgy, not an appendage, it is dance felt as experience—the dance reminiscent of first-century Christians.

What is the future of the dance in Christianity? Its place in Christian worship is indicated by its history—a rich and exciting history of which unfortunately many are unaware. Through the work of contemporary Church dancers more people are coming to know and appreciate this tradition. The value of physical movement and expression has only recently come to be understood as the teaching of movement awareness schools has been expounded. As the twentieth century draws to a close there are increasing indications that the time is ripe for a reawakening of the use of the dance in Christian liturgy—a dance which is both historically rooted and grounded in contemporary validity.

Notes

1. Rudolf Laban, *The Mastery of Movement* (Boston: Plays Inc., 1971), p. 5.

2. Walter Sorell, *The Dance Through the Ages* (New York: Grosset & Dunlap, 1967), p. 19.

3. W. O. E. Oesterley, *The Sacred Dance* (New York: Dance Horizons Inc., 1923), p. 35.

4. W. G. Raffe assisted by M. E. Purdon, *Dictionary of The Dance* (New York: A. S. Barnes & Co., 1964), p. 251.

5. Laban, p. 96.

6. Paul Tillich, *Theology of Culture* (New York: Oxford University Press, 1959), p. 56.

7. Evelyn Underhill, *Worship* (New York: Harper Brothers, 1936), p. 100.

8. Brad Thompson, ed., *Liturgies of the Western World* (Cleveland: World, 1961), p. 37.

9. Doug Adams, *Modern Liturgy,* Vol. 4, No. 3, March 1977, p. 2.

10. Curt Sachs, *World History of the Dance* (New York: W. W. Norton & Co. Inc., 1963), p. 144.

11. G. R. S. Mead, *The Sacred Dance In Christendom* (London: John W. Watkins, 1926), p. 65.

12. Eusebius DVC, xi.

13. E. Louis Backman, *Religious Dances in the Christian Church and in Popular Medicine* (London: Allen & Unwin, 1952), p. 24.

14. *Ibid.,* p. 25.

15. Ambrose, *Commentary on the Gospel of St. Luke,* p. vi.

16. Sorell, p. 36.

17. Chrysostom, *Hom. i.* (In illud, vidi Dom.) 1.

18. Augustine, *Speech* (cccxi).

19. Theodoret, *Graecarum Affectionum Curatio* (xi).

20. Margaret Fisk Taylor, *A Time To Dance: Symbolic Movement in Worship* (Philadelphia: United Church Press, 1967), p. 84.

21. Backman, p. 77.

22. Raffe, p. 452.

23. Taylor, p. 86.

24. Maria-Gabriele Wosien, *Sacred Dance: Encounter with the Gods* (New York: Avon Books, 1974), p. 27.

25. Lincoln Kirstein, *The Book of the Dance* (New York: Garden City Publishing Co., Inc., 1942), p. 91.

26. R. Kraus, *History of the Dance in Art and Education* (Englewood Cliffs: Prentice-Hall, Inc., 1969), p. 50.

27. Backman, p. 52.

28. *Ibid.,* p. 85.

29. *Analecta Hymnica* (Leipzig, 1890), p. 2, 62.

30. *Ibid.,* pp. 1, 207.

31. *Ibid.,* pp. 53, 97.

32. E. Jacobs, *Rosengarten im deutschen Lied, Land, und Brauch* (Halle, 1897).

33. *Analecta Hymnica,* pp. 16, 72.

34. *Ibid.,* pp. 20, 178.

35. *Planctus of Cividale del Fruili* (Reale Museo Archeologico: Cividalenso Saec. xiv, foll.), p. 74.

36. Kirstein, p. 76

37. Renee Foatelli, *Les Danses Religieuses dans le Christianisme* (Paris: Editions Spes, 1947), p. 95.

38. Bonaventura, *Dieta Salutis* (Autreus Libellus, 1260).

39. Mead, p. 253.

40. Barbara W. Tuchman, *A Distant Mirror, The Calamitous 14th Century* (New York: Alfred A. Knopf, 1978), p. 532.

41. Shakespeare, *Romeo and Juliet* (Act IV, Scene IV).

42. Kirstein, p. 85.

43. Sachs, p. 252.

44. Backman, pp. 135–136.

45. Henri Stegemeier, *The Dance of Death in Folk Song* (Chicago: University of Chicago Libraries, 1939), p. 6.

46. Ellsmere, *Daunce of Death* (MS. LXIII-LXIV).

47. Kirstein, p. 87.

48. *Ibid.,* p. 88.

49. Backman, p. 191.

50. Paul Nettl, *The Story of Dance Music* (New York: Philosophical Library, 1947), p. 44.

51. G. G. Coulton, *The Medieval Scene* (London: Cambridge University Press, 1967), p. 20.

52. Dante, *Divine Comedy* (Paradise VII).

53. Ethel Urlin, *Dancing, Ancient and Modern* (New York: Appleton & Co., 1914), p. 44.

54. Florence Whyte, *The Dance of Death in Spain and Catalonia* (New York: Arno Press, 1977), p. 42.

55. Kirstein, p. 117.

56. *Ibid.,* p. 139.

57. Roland Bainton, *The Martin Luther Christmas Book* (Philadelphia: Westminster Press, 1948), p. 76.

58. Taylor, p. 108.

59. Louis Horst, *Pre-Classic Dance Forms* (New York: Dance Observer, 1937), p. 7.

60. Thoinot Arbeau, *Orchesography* (London: Beaumont, 1925), p. 19.

61. Eric Blom, ed., *Grove's Dictionary of Music and Musicians* (New York: St. Martin's Press, 1954), p. 48.

62. Mead, p. 258.

63. Johannes Boemus, *Omniumo Gentium Mores Leges et Ritus* (1520 fol. 58b.).

64. Backman, p. 37.

65. Menestrier, *Des Ballet Anciens et Modernes* (Paris, 1682).

66. "Letter of John Cotton to R Levitt," *Collections* (Mass. Historical Society, Series 2, Vol. X, 1823), p. 183.

67. Increase Mather, *An Arrow Against Profane and Promiscuous Dancing, Drawn Out of the Quiver of the Scriptures, By the Ministers*

of Christ at Boston in New England (Boston: Samuel Green, 1684), p. 1.

68. Percy A. Scholes, *The Puritans and Music in England and New England* (New York: Russell & Russell Inc., 1962), p. 248.

69. Taylor, p. 124.

70. E. D. Andrews, "The Dancer in Shaker Ritual," in *Chronicles of The American Dance* (New York: Henry Holt & Co., 1948), p. 4.

71. *Ibid.,* p. 10.

72. Taylor, p. 127.

73. *Ibid.,* p. 126.

74. Roderyk Lange, *The Nature of The Dance* (New York: International Publications Service, 1976), p. 10.

75. Ralph Adams Cram, "How Shall We Worship God?" unpublished ms. in Boston Public Library, Cram Collection.

76. Ronald Knox, *The Mass in Slow Motion* (New York: Sheed & Ward, 1948), pp. 110–112.